What Every

NAZARENE
BOARD
MEMBER

Needs to Know

What Every

NAZARENE BOARD MEMBER

Needs to Know

Leslie Parrott Sr.

NAZARENE PUBLISHING HOUSE
Kansas City, Missouri

Copyright 1995
by Nazarene Publishing House

ISBN 083-411-5506

Printed in the
United States of America

Cover design: Art Jacobs/Ted Ferguson

10 9 8 7 6 5 4 3 2 1

This book is dedicated
to the church board
of the
Puyallup, Washington,
Church of the Nazarene.

CONTENTS

PREFACE

THE CHURCH OF THE NAZARENE is committed to a representative form of government with built-in checks and balances. As one church leader said, "We believe in strong leadership, but the people have the last word."

The Church of the Nazarene is led by strong, God-called ministers who serve in their various assignments, including—but not exclusively—pastors, district superintendents, general superintendents, denominational executives, institutional presidents, and missionaries.

Every pastor works with lay leaders on the church board, plus committees and councils who make up the organizational structure of the local church. At every other level in the church, designated leaders work with a combination of laypersons and clergypersons who make up the boards, committees, and councils on districts, regions, and in the structure of the general church headquarters.

Clergy leaders are captains of their ships, but it is the boards, committees, and councils who provide steam in the boilers. They provide the thrust that supports leadership. They provide the budgets and approve the personnel leadership needs for their programs and projects.

Spiritual, financial, and numerical progress in the local church depends heavily on the quality of relationship the pastor and staff have with their lay leaders on the boards, councils, and committees in the congregation. The relationship of the pastor with the church board is often the defining point in his leadership.

This book is especially dedicated to helping church boards orient themselves to the governance process. As a corollary, there may also be help for persons serving on the important councils and committees of the church.

The boards, councils, and committees listed in the Local Government section of the *Manual of the Church of the Nazarene* are as follows:

- Church Board
- Evangelism and Church Membership Committee
- Nominating Committee
- Education Committee
- Sunday School Ministries Board
- Committee of the Board to Monitor the Budget
- Committee of the Board to Count and Account for All Money
- Auditing Committee
- Long-range Planning Committee
- Stewards
- Trustees
- Local Stewardship Committee
- Children's Ministries Council
- Adult Ministries Council
- Nazarene Youth International Council
- Nazarene Youth International Executive Committee
- Nazarene Youth International Nominating Committee
- Nazarene World Mission Society Council
- Nazarene World Mission Society Executive Committee
- Nazarene World Mission Society Nominating Committee

These 20 boards, councils, and committees detailed in the *Manual* do not include the variety of standing committees and special committees of the church board. By the sheer weight of their numbers, it seems the time is at hand to provide pastors and laymen with tools for refining the important governance work the church has called them to do.

What Every

NAZARENE
BOARD
MEMBER

Needs to Know

1

The Birth of the Board

 The purpose of this chapter is to tell the story and then analyze the development of the Nazarene church board under the leadership of Dr. P. F. Bresee.

THE RONALD REAGAN STATE BUILDING now stands on the exact site of the storefront structure at 317 South Main Street in Los Angeles where dedicated Christians met to organize a congregation called the "Church of the Nazarene" on October 30, 1895. The minutes say their purpose for gathering was "to elect officers and begin the necessary steps to incorporate" their new church.

Their mission and vision were clear: "Feeling clearly called of God for the carrying on of His work in the conversion of sinners, the sanctification of believers, and the building up in holiness of those who may be committed to our care, we associate ourselves together as a church of God under the name of the Church of the Nazarene."

The new church's mission and vision were a matter of consensus. The pastors, J. P. Widney and Phineas Bresee, and the congregation, all former members of other churches, knew who they were and why they were forming a new Protestant body: "We seek the simplicity and Pentecostal power of the primitive New Testament Church."

They identified the people they expected to serve: "The field of labor to which we feel especially called is in the neglected quarters of the cities and where ever else may be found the waste places and the souls seeking pardon and cleansing from sin."

In keeping with today's "vision statements," they put their strategy in writing. "This work we aim to do through the agency of city missions, evangelistic services, house-to-house visitation, caring for the poor, and comforting the dying; to this end we strive personally to walk with God and to incite others so to do."

Provisions were made to establish a local church board during this same meeting. First, they arranged to elect trustees "who may receive and hold and transfer property for that congregation, but who shall not transfer real estate without a consenting vote of two-thirds of the membership of that congregation."

The minutes also say: "There shall be no less than five and no more than seven Stewards . . . who shall have special charge of the current expenses of the congregation."

In these statements concerning the duties of trustees and stewards, the pastors and the congregation clarified the division of labor between the clergy and the church board. Subsequent minutes show that the board saw their pastors, Bresee and Widney, as their leaders with authority in all matters relating to worship, evangelism, outreach, nurturing, and the like.

However, the board and the pastors seemed to function with a collegial relationship on those matters that fell between the board's responsibility for business and finance on the one hand and the pastors' responsibility for spiritual leadership on the other. For instance, the board authorized the appointment of a lady to do follow-up work with new converts, but Bresee seemed to have a free hand in setting revival dates, calling the workers, and raising the revival finances. They followed the pattern of Acts

6, in which seven men chosen by the church did "serve tables," while the apostles gave themselves "to prayer, and to the ministry of the word" (KJV).

Bresee, Widney, and their church faced issues that are still contemporary. The minutes say, "We recognize the equal rights of both men and women to all offices of the church, including the ministry." Did they envision ministry in a denomination that might someday supersede the single congregation in Los Angeles?

Five nights later, on Monday, November 4, 1895, the first official meeting of the first church board in the Church of the Nazarene was held in Widney's office on West First Street in Los Angeles. In keeping with the terms of the founding charter, one of the pastors presided.

This group separated spiritual leadership from the secular responsibilities that the church required. The pastor was the spiritual leader of the church with a free hand to lead, while property matters and financing were the prerogatives of the board.

At their first board meeting, they elected a secretary, treasurer, and financial secretary. The financial secretary was responsible for counting and banking money, while the treasurer wrote checks. The organizers foresaw the tendency of a treasurer to assume a proprietary attitude toward the bank account: "It was moved and passed that the treasurer should pay out money only on order of the official board; signed and attested to by the secretary."

The board authorized the reimbursement of 70 cents for the purchase of a ledger book. They further authorized $3.30 for advertising and $14.00 for filing the corporation papers. The treasurer was instructed to pay the $30.00 rent each month "until further notice." One dollar was budgeted for the janitor.

The board voted to pay Bresee's first month's salary of

$125. Payment of his salary was an agenda item for several months until it was authorized on an "until further notice" basis. Bresee's first raise came five years later, when his salary was increased from $125 to $150 monthly.

The usual form of later board meetings was to first hear the report of the financial secretary on income and then listen to the report of the treasurer on bills paid and the current bank balance. Only then did they take up new bills.

By all accounts between 1895 and 1912, the church did not live from hand to mouth but kept financial arrangements in good order. There was no pastor's report or any regular agenda items relating to his work. Matters of church program took a backseat to finance and property management because of their evident tendency to leave all spiritual leadership and guidance in the hands of their pastor.

The second big but not exclusive concern of the board was the church property. In December the board authorized the purchase of torches for street meetings, professional lettering on the church bulletin board, and a small amount of money for printing. Bresee was reimbursed $4.00 for the tuning of the piano, which he had paid for, and $5.75 to Mr. W. S. Knott for the fuel oil he had bought. Apparently it was common practice to pay bills personally and seek reimbursement. In the March meeting, "the Building Committee was authorized to purchase an outside lamp and have it placed in front of the building."

However, in the meeting of March 1896, they moved ahead on a plan for follow-up on converts: "On motion, Mrs. Craft was appointed to provide the names and addresses of the new converts as they were converted and to generally look after them, and in the association of others with her as she might need." They also voted to hold "a campfire on the first Monday night in April" to celebrate the first six months of their existence as a church.

The board used committees for almost everything. Most of these committees were appointed ad hoc for the specific purpose indicated and then dissolved when their work was done. For instance: A committee chose the lamp and installed it in front of the church. Another committee was appointed "to decide on a suitable coal for the church and purchase a half ton as they might deem best, and on their direction, the treasurer ordered to pay for same." They appointed a committee on membership revision, a Sunday School committee, an auditing committee, a district advisory board, and a committee to "arrange suitable cards" for the Christmas feast Bresee planned as a holiday event. By current standards, the board micromanaged the church finances and did do so until at least 1912.

The pastors had a free hand in the spiritual leadership of the church. There are no indications of any second guessing of their leadership or controlling pastoral decisions.

For instance, at the end of one meeting, "Dr. Bresee stated that he had invited Brother Hendricks to come and supply the pulpit for three Sabbaths in October." The action was approved, and "arrangements were referred to the Committee on Pastoral Relations," a committee who apparently served the pastor without controlling him.

"At the end" of another meeting, Bresee reported that Dr. C. J. Fowler, who had held a revival, had been paid $325 compensation "for his services and his traveling expenses." There was no indication in previous minutes that the board authorized the meetings, the dates, the choice of evangelist, or even his pay. The pay was probably a love offering, and the rest of the decisions were those of Bresee and Widney.

In the board meeting of February 1, 1897, Bresee reported: "To the official board of the Church of the Nazarene, Los Angeles, Calif. I would like to report that after a 10-day meeting at Berkeley, Calif., I organized a church with 19 members with Earnest A. Girvin as pastor and George W. Agelston, associate pastor, both having been duly chosen by the church and approved by the superintendents . . . this is the second Church of the Nazarene."

The First Church *Manual*

The role of the pastor and the church board were made clear in the 1903 *Manual of the Church of the Nazarene.* By this time Widney had resigned, and Bresee was the senior pastor with an associate. *First,* the pastor was the designated leader of the church. "The special duties of elders, in addition to the conducting of public worship and the preaching of the gospel, shall be the administration of the church."

In the same *Manual,* the role of the trustees was made equally clear. "The Board of Trustees . . . shall hold all church property, and shall be amenable to the Church Board . . . and that the secular affairs of such corporation shall be managed and controlled by a Board of Trustees elected and organized according to the provisions of said *Manual.*"

The role of the church board (summarized on page 40 of the *Manual*), was "for the general business of the congregation . . . the pastor being ex-officio President."

The role of the stewards to "have special charge of the expenses of the congregation" later evolved to the current idea of stewards as servants of the Lord helping the poor and needy, nurturing the congregation, and providing the elements for the Lord's Supper, all under the invitation and supervision of the pastor.

The Church Board 12 Years Later

The First General Assembly of the Pentecostal Church of the Nazarene was historic. It was held in Chicago in 1907. There the Church of the Nazarene merged with the Association of Pentecostal Churches of America, an Eastern denomination whose New England roots went back to 1887. The next year the Pentecostal Church of the Nazarene merged with the Holiness Church of Christ, from the South, at another historic assembly in Pilot Point, Tex.

The statements in the 1907 *Manual* clearly define the relationship between the pastor and the board:

The pastor's leadership was laid down clearly:

The Pastor has general oversight of the Church of which he is in charge. All departments are under his care and supervision. He is ex-officio chairman of the Church Board. He is to make regular reports to the District Superintendent. He is to preach the Word. He is to visit from house to house, conversing and praying with the people, imitating the example of the Apostle Paul, who said, "By the space of three years I ceased not to warn every one, night and day, with tears." . . . [He is to] build . . . up believers in holiness.

This was the beginning of a very good job description for pastors serving churches in that era. (1) The pastor had general oversight. (2) He or she was accountable for the money. (3) The pastor was to chair the board meeting. (4) He or she made regular reports to the district superintendent, although nothing is said about the pastor reporting to the church board. (5) The pastor was to visit in the homes and (6) carry a burden for the people.

The Manual *also states that stewards*

shall be members of the Church Board, . . . who may, when necessary, assist the Elders in the distribution of the elements at the sacrament of the Lord's Supper.

. . . The Stewards shall co-operate with the Deaconesses in seeking the needy and distressed in order to relieve and comfort them . . . and as shall be necessary, to exhort to greater liberality to meet the requirements of the Church.

Thus, the fundamental role of stewards to help the needy and nurture the congregation was in place by 1907. It has not substantively changed.

The role of the trustees was similar, in essence, to the responsibilities of trustees today.

The Trustees . . . shall hold all Church property, and shall be amenable to the Church . . . In no case shall the Trustees mortgage or encumber the real estate for the current expenses of the Church. . . . the secular affairs of such corporation shall be managed and controlled by a Board of Trustees.

The work of most Boards of Trustees is focused on the property and its financing. The "secular affairs" they were to manage must have been the church property, its upkeep, cleaning, and financing.

On pages 48-51 in the 1907 Manual, *the duties of the church board are*

to have charge of the general business of the congregation . . . ; to keep an exact account of all moneys received for the support of the pastors and the current expenses of the Church; to make an accurate report of every expenditure . . . To license proper persons to preach the Gospel who have been recommended by the pastor . . . To recommend preachers for election to orders . . . To approve Sunday School Superintendents, and to appoint a Sunday School Committee . . . To call a pastor for the oversight and care of the Church . . . To provide for the support and the moving expenses of the pastor thus called. To secure suitable books for the keeping of the records of all official meetings, for Church membership and financial accounts. . . . The Church Board shall appoint a Church Membership Committee . . . whose duty it shall be to recommend to the pastor persons for Church membership.

This list of church board duties in 1907 empowered the pastor to do his or her work. The pastor was not under the control of the board but worked with it, providing strong spiritual leadership to the congregation. The pastor was not a chief executive officer (CEO) who preached on Sunday, nor was the board a hiring, firing, controlling entity. All were brothers and sisters in the family of God, working together for one purpose. In those days they referred to each other as "Brother" and "Sister." Even the pastor was a "Brother" or "Sister."

The Legacy of This Early Church Board

Bresee, Widney, and their lay associates set out terms and conditions for the church board in the charter for the church in Los Angeles in 1895. By 1907, 12 years later, the role of the board and the relationship of pastor and board to one another had changed, partly through evolution and partly through merger, into a philosophy of boardmanship that resembles much that is in the *Manual of the Church of the Nazarene* today.

All the wealth of church management literature, the philosophies of church growth, Sunday School promotion, and the like was yet to come. But with all the development and study of church growth and church management, the board has been left on its own, to build on the legacy left by our pioneers.

The Church of the Nazarene has inherited a legacy on the role of the pastor's relationship with the church board. Its most fundamental points are as follows:

1. The pastor is the designated leader of the church.
2. Church boards are important.
3. The responsibilities of the church board include the management of church facilities, control of church finances, and cooperation with the pastor on program development.
4. There is a necessary separation of spiritual leadership from the management of the church's secular affairs.
5. The pastor is responsible for the administration of the church.
6. Early church board philosophy assumed spiritually mature persons on the board.

Times are not the same now as they were in 1895 or even in 1912. But the philosophy that divides spiritual and business leadership in the Nazarene Church is still applicable. The only thing contemporary times have added is the pastor's cellular phone and the board's computer printouts. The Los Angeles Church's division of labor was learned from the Church in Jerusalem in A.D. 30. It works well today.

2

The Business of the Board

 *The purpose of this chapter is to ex-
plain the purpose of the church board.*

THE TITLE FOR THIS CHAPTER refers to the section in
the *Manual of the Church of the Nazarene* called The Business of the Church Board. Some people are confused
about the business of the board. Some think the pastor is
the employee of the board and that the board attitude toward him or her should reflect this perception. Others see
the pastor as the ordained, God-called, spiritual leader
who has been sent to shepherd the congregation and
therefore deserves a free hand with minimum accountability. Between these two extremes is the rational ground
described best as *relationship,* a very important word in a
board that sees their pastor as a colleague and leader.

Since the church board's work is with their pastor,
there is a direct relationship between the quality of that
alliance and the effectiveness of the board. To the degree
the relationship between the pastor and the board is positive and productive, morale in the congregation is propor-
tionately high. And for every centimeter of tarnish on that
relationship, morale drops and effectiveness fades. If the
pastor and the board enter into conflict over who has control, morale falls through the floor, and an adversarial relationship results.

Besides the primary relationship with their pastor,
the board also have a "sometimes" relationship with the

district superintendent, an ongoing relationship with members of the congregation, a continuing relationship with each other, and conceivably a relationship with a general superintendent during special circumstances. But none of these relationships competes with the importance of the pastor and the board working together agreeably.

Collaboration and Cooperation

By definition, a relationship is the state of affairs between people who have dealings with each other. Or to put it another way, relationship is the social condition that describes the connection between persons who, for whatever reason, are associated together.

Everyone has relationships. Drivers and filling station operators have a relationship. Husbands and wives have a relationship. Employers and employees have a relationship. Teachers and pupils have a relationship. And one thing is for sure: pastors and church boards have a relationship. The quality of that relationship determines everything else.

A good relationship may be described by such words as *happy, productive, beneficial, relaxed,* and *trusting.* A bad relationship may be described by such words as *strained, cheerless, sour, caustic,* and *hopeless.* The reader may observe that each of the words used to describe the good or bad relationship between the pastor and the board comes from a mind-set or attitude. And the most elementary student of human understanding knows that each of us is responsible for his or her own attitudes. An attitude is a matter of choice.

To further advance this understanding of the all-important relationship of the pastor with the church board, two words that look and sound similar need to be explained. *Cooperation* and *collaboration* are often used interchangeably—but they are conceptually different. Co-operation comes primarily from the *heart*. Collaboration is primarily a matter of the *head*.

A *cooperative* board member is one who affiliates closely or warmly with the pastor and other board members. The *cooperative* pastor is one who identifies with the feelings of the board, who has enough empathy to put himself or herself into the shoes of board members and enough willingness to see and feel things from their point of view. A cooperative pastor and board find it easy to accommodate each other. Their positive feelings for one another are mutual even when they disagree.

Collaboration is not divorced from feeling but is more a matter of the mind. In *collaboration*, the emphasis is on doing or achieving, and accomplishing things together. A professional basketball team may collaborate for the purposes of winning the game when there is little spirit of cooperation among them or even with the coach. Collaboration comes from a Latin word meaning "to labor together" or "to work together toward a common end."

In *The Music Man* is a song about people in Iowa who "can stand toe-to-toe for days and days and never see eye-to-eye." But the good people of Iowa can work together whether or not they see eye to eye. In the musical, they worked together at the task of saving their children from degradation, even though the spirit of cooperation among themselves was in short supply. Such is the spirit of the British, who call the political party out of office "the Queen's loyal opposition."

Cooperation and collaboration work in tandem within the board. The ideal pastor-board relationship melds the spirit or attitude of cooperation and the teamwork required for collaboration. The distinction is an important fine line.

The Power of the Old Guard

Every mature church has within it a group known lovingly as "the old guard," lay leaders with time on their side. They have been around long enough to play leading roles in the story of the church, and they have stature. Many other church people take them as reference points on important church matters. Their power can be considerable.

A businessman took me to his country club for lunch, where he told me an unforgettable story. His church had called a promising young man in his mid-30s to pastor their congregation. The new pastor had grown up in a parsonage, attended a Nazarene college, and graduated from Nazarene Theological Seminary. He was obviously gifted. The whole church was excited.

However, the pastor had not been on his new assignment more than six months when much of the enthusiasm from the board had turned to disappointment. As my friend said, "The old guard who had run the church for years realized we had made a mistake." The young man was bright but arrogant. He said inappropriate things from the pulpit. He was obviously much more concerned about how *he* was doing than how *they* were doing. His tendency toward Christian materialism set the teeth of the board on edge. A radical change in staffing was the last straw. Furthermore, he had new ideas and would fiercely stomp on those who resisted him. He was an easy subject of rumors.

From across the table, my layman friend said, "We were on the spot. What could we do?

"Then," he said, "the most influential member of our board invited five or six of us to breakfast on a Saturday morning. After we talked and laughed together, he became solemn at the end of the meal. This man at the head of the table was the leading layman in that church. He was a respected member of the old guard. Others tended to take his lead on things.

"Leaning forward in his chair, the older man said, 'I think you know why we are here. We have a problem we hate to face. We have a new pastor, and it isn't working very well. Maybe we made a mistake. But I've been thinking and praying a lot about this, and I just felt we should get together and talk.'

"Sweeping the table with his eyes, he continued. 'We have two options as I see it. We can either *accept him* like he is, or we can *attack him* for not being what we thought we were getting. If we attack him, it will take two or three years to get rid of him. And we can do it. However, I keep thinking about the people who will be hurt in the process, especially the young people and those who see something in him that we don't.

"'Or,' he said, 'we can take another approach. We can accept him like he is instead of the way we thought he was going to be. We can make a decision among ourselves to communicate to him in all the ways we know how—that he is not on trial. We can let him know he is not under suspicion. He is our pastor, and we can learn to love him without waiting for his ways to match our expectations. If we take this tack, he may eventually mature; or later on, when the timing is right, we can help him leave with his head up, and neither he nor the church will be damaged.'"

My friend said, "Everything was silent—really still. Then one man spoke up, and then another. Around the table, each man said it in his own way, but we all came down on the side of choosing to love and support the pastor we had thought God was sending us when we voted to call him."

Then my friend came to the climax of his story. He explained, "That was 13 years ago last summer. Our pastor is still here. We love him as a board. He is loved by our congregation. And in the meantime he has matured like you can't believe. We have a new sanctuary that was a long-time dream of the congregation. Our membership has far more than doubled. And all I ever hear from the pastor is that he wants to stay here for the rest of his life. I guess he was a late bloomer, and we were about to give up on him too soon."

As he was signing the tab for lunch, my friend interrupted the procedure with an appendage to his story. "I don't think any one of those men has ever told anyone about that Saturday morning breakfast. And I break the silence only because you are studying church boards, and I wanted you to hear what happened to us."

Unfortunately, I know another story about a pastor and a disappointed church—but this story has a different ending. A young pastor accepted a call from a congregation where it was soon obvious to him that the board was disappointed. Their comparisons with his predecessor were never favorable. He tried to build good relationships, and I am sure they did too, at least in the beginning. But nothing seemed to work. Somewhere along the line the old guard decided to *attack* him instead of *accept* him.

It was three years before the pastor finally left. But the process of getting rid of him was disastrous. The story is littered with quotes and misquotes, misperceptions, happenings lifted out of context, and rumors repeated as facts. In the end, the people thought he could do nothing right. When a server dropped a Communion plate, it was the pastor's fault. The church lost many families. Hurt feelings spread like malaria. The pastor now leads another congregation who accepts him, and he loves them. But all the while he strives to nurse his own scars and those of his family. Everyone lost.

The 46 Duties of a Nazarene Board

A review of the Church Board section, as well as other paragraphs in the Local Government section of the *Manual of the Church of the Nazarene,* suggests 46 duties of the church board. The list is given here in common talk to avoid the legalese of the more precise language in the *Manual.* Since this material is provided for church board orientation, it may be appropriate to study the matter more deeply later, when the time is appropriate.

1. Approve the Nominating Committee.
2. Organize itself into committees.
3. Nominate a new pastor.
4. Communicate pastoral goals and expectations in writing.
5. Set the pastor's remuneration.
6. Cover costs of the new pastor's move.
7. Submit controversy on a pastoral call to the general superintendent.
8. Accept the resignation of the pastor.
9. Receive a current membership roll from the outgoing pastor.
10. Seek reconciliation of differences in the church.
11. Review pastoral relations with the district superintendent.
12. Call for "special pastoral review" if necessary.
13. Call special church meetings if necessary.
14. Set a monthly meeting date.
15. Care for the interests of the church.
16. Conduct a self-study.
17. Arrange for pastoral supply between pastors.
18. Develop and adopt an annual budget.
19. Monitor the budget.

20. Provide financial arrangements for support of the pastor and staff.
21. Be alert to the continuing education needs of the pastor and staff.
22. Set support for evangelists.
23. Consider the support needs of the district superintendent and the general superintendents.
24. License local and lay ministers.
25. Recommend those desiring certificates for assigned roles of ministry to the district assembly.
26. Recommend licensed ministers to the district assembly.
27. Recommend persons for renewal of deaconess' licenses at district assembly.
28. Elect a director of children's ministries.
29. Elect a director of adult ministries.
30. Approve the election of the NYI president.
31. Approve administrators of church day schools.
32. Elect a secretary.
33. Elect a treasurer.
34. Make careful accounting of all money received and disbursed.
35. Provide a committee to count and account for all money received.
36. Appoint an auditing committee.
37. Provide an evangelism and membership committee.
38. Serve, in some instances, as the Sunday School Ministries Board.
39. Decide in a new church when a Sunday School superintendent will be elected.
40. Appoint a trial committee if a member faces written charges.

41. Elect all paid staff members.
42. Elect all unpaid staff.
43. Provide for long-range planning.
44. Follow denominational plans for paying budgets.
45. Remove inactive members from the roll.
46. Hold all official documents in trust.

Duties of the Stewards

Besides the general duties of the church board, the *Manual* spells out the responsibilities of both the stewards and the trustees. Following the biblical example in Acts 6:1-3 and Rom. 12:6-8, stewards are to see their duties as to minister, not administrate. Their duties are summarized as follows:

1. Serve as a church growth committee.
2. Serve as the Evangelism and Church Membership Committee.
3. Serve the needs of the poor and distressed.
4. Assist the pastor in organizing work for volunteers.
5. Serve as liaisons in community service.
6. Assist the pastor in nurturing the congregation.
7. Provide elements for the Lord's Supper.
8. Promote the cause of Christian stewardship.

Duties of the Trustees

The duties of the trustees are as assigned by the board. But all their responsibilities relate to property and financing. Their duties are summarized as follows:

1. Hold title to the church property and manage it in some circumstances.
2. Be available when needed for construction and financial planning.
3. Attend to the raising of funds that keep the pastor free from secular care.

Observations on Duties of the Church Board

1. *All board duties are important but not of equal value and concern.*

• The most important duties of the board are in pastoral relations: These include the process of (1) prayerfully choosing a new pastor, (2) learning to work productively with him or her, and then (3) reviewing his or her service and leadership. If these duties are fulfilled well, everything else the board does will follow naturally.

• The next important duty of the board is to ensure the integrity of the church. Integrity usually relates to money matters and the character and accountability of personnel.

• The third top priority in board work is adequate planning. The term *strategic planning* intimidates some boards, but it need not. If you plan to pay your budgets next year, how do you intend to do it? That is strategic planning. Otherwise, the goal of paying all the budgets is just good intentions.

• The fourth high priority of the board is to keep all relationships in good repair. The primary relationship of the board is with the pastor. But other important relationships include the following: (1) the congregation and concerned constituencies within the congregation, such as seniors, teens, musicians, and the like; (2) denominational authorities, especially the district superintendent; (3) volunteers (the church would shut down if it were not for unpaid lay workers who keep the wheels turning); (4) the community (it is the business of the board to see that the church is integrated into the community); (5) the pastor's children (the parsonage family members are related to the church like no other family; and recognition of the unique role of the pastor's family can go a long way in motivating the pastor).

2. *The church board does its work primarily under the leadership of the pastor.*

• The board works with the district superintendent in calling a pastor. In fact, the superintendent has veto power in the choice of a new pastor and, in some cases, may even appoint a pastor. But in most instances, calling a new pastor is a cooperative venture of the church board, led by the district superintendent.

• The pastor is the official chairman of the board. In most states he or she is also chairman of the nonprofit corporation, which is the congregation's legal entity. He or she signs all legal documents.

Although there is no mention in the *Manual* of a lay chairman of the board or lay chairman of the trustees, some boards elect a lay chairman as the recognized lay leader of the congregation. Unofficially, the lay chairman serves (1) as a "lightning rod" for people with problems, (2) as an advocate for the pastor and his or her family, and (3) as a spokesman for the laity on ceremonial occasions.

• The board has no authority to call a meeting on its own. This is the prerogative of the pastor or district superintendent, or the church secretary with the permission of the pastor or district superintendent.

• The authority of individual board members is restricted to times when the board is in session or for doing specific tasks assigned by the board. Board members do not act on their own.

3. *It might be a good idea for board members to be delegates to the district assembly, even though the* Manual *is silent on the matter.*

4. *Although the duties of the pastor are listed in the* Manual, *further implications can be drawn.*

• The pastor is the spiritual leader of the church, with

considerable latitude in organizing his or her own time and work.

• The pastor leads the worship services and chooses his or her preaching themes as the Spirit guides, usually in harmony with local congregational needs, expectations, and traditions.

• The availability of the pastor to the people and the accountability of his or her time will eventually become apparent. There is limited *Manual* authority on how these matters will be worked out between the pastor and the board. But boards like to feel their pastor works hard and uses time well.

The minutes of the district assembly spell the terms of vacation (length) but not the conditions (when and in what time segments). Office hours, visitation, study time, and so on are left to the pastor's own values and priorities. No two ministers discipline themselves the same.

• The great gray area of the pastor's work habits and time management makes it all the more important that the board and the pastor develop a good working relationship.

• The *Manual* has made the pastor directly accountable to the board on matters of finance and subject to the authority of the entire congregation on matters of real estate purchases, sales, and mortgages.

5. *There are three fundamental statements addressed to both pastors and boards that deserve special attention.*

• *First,* under the *Manual* section on the Calling of a Pastor, there is the directive: "The church board and the pastor should clearly communicate their goals and expectations to each other in writing" (115.2).

This document is like the North Star. It becomes the reference point for drawing the map the pastor and board will follow in reaching where they have agreed to go. This document also serves all parties well in the reviewing process at the end of the year or at the time of the pastoral review with the district superintendent.

• *Second,* under the *Manual* section The Pastor/Church Relationship is the statement: "At least every other year, the pastor and the church board shall conduct a self-study to review the expectations, goals, and performance of the church and pastor" (120).

A good self-study consists of three sections: (1) This is where we are now. (2) This is where we would like to be next year or the year after. (3) These are the things we plan to do together to get there. Only measurable goals are useful.

• *Third,* there is a formula for solving differences. Every organization needs a due-process procedure to follow when things turn sour. The *Manual* has provided a specific plan for dealing with differences and the more serious conflicts that afflict churches on occasion:

> Pastors and congregations shall seek a clear understanding of each others' expectations and sincerely follow biblical principles to resolve differences in a spirit of reconciliation within the church. Biblical principles for resolving differences in Matthew 18:15-20 and Galatians 6:1-5 include:
>
> (1) Seek to resolve differences by discussing them face-to-face.
>
> (2) If face-to-face discussion fails to bring resolution, seek the assistance of one or two others in resolving the differences.
>
> (3) Bring the differences to the church board only after face-to-face discussion and small-group efforts fail.
>
> (4) Christians are obligated to work at resolving differences in a spirit of love, acceptance, and forgiveness. (120.2)

6. *The most fundamental concept in the governance of the congregation and the administration of the church is the idea of checks and balances.*

Almost everything the pastor or church board is authorized to do is checked by the other. Here are a few examples of these checks and balances: (1) When the pastor is authorized to appoint the Nominating Committee, the board is given the right of approval. (2) The pastor nominates staff, but the board elects and the pastor supervises. (3) The board is authorized to provide for a long-range planning committee, but the pastor is the ex officio chairman. (4) "The church board together with the pastor shall" raise the budget money.

The only time the board does business without the pastor is when the church is between pastors. But then they work with the district superintendent, who has the authority of a veto if the process gets out of control. When the new pastor arrives, it is back to the checks and balances of the pastor-board relationship.

There is no place where this joint assignment concept is clearer than in the directive concerning Business under the *Manual* section on the Church Board.

The business of the board is "to care for the interests of the church . . . in harmony with the pastor" (129.1). This statement from the *Manual* brings us back full circle. A good working relationship between the pastor and the board is of absolute importance. This is their consummate duty.

3

The Advantages of
Better Board Arrangements

The purpose of this chapter is to describe good arrangements for church board meetings.

ALTHOUGH THE BUSINESS of the church board is defined in some detail in the *Manual of the Church of the Nazarene,* arrangements for the meetings are not. This silence makes way for positive, creative means for making the meetings smoother and potentially more effective because of good arrangements.

How Many Meetings Are Enough?

The *Manual* prescribes 12 monthly meetings of the local church board, to be scheduled during the first 15 days of each month. If the board endeavors to act as one mind in a hands-on administration of the church, 12 meetings may not be enough. Pastors who look to their boards as the "church administrator" are continually calling impromptu meetings to address an incessant flow of consequential and inconsequential problems that call for decisions.

Boards who meet numerous times in an effort to fill their administrative role are likely to blur their vision and confuse important decisions with inconsequential ones. All decisions are necessary, but not all decisions are of equal importance.

Repairing the organ is an administrative decision. Circumstance does not change that fact. The decision to repair may be made by the church in a regular monthly meeting, an impromptu after-church meeting in the choir loft, or by the pastor under a board policy that calls for keeping the instruments in good repair. It is a misuse of board time and resources to make administrative decisions unless the board has chosen to be the church administrator. In that case, it is hard to have too many meetings.

If the church board plans the year with a realistic budget document, an annual calendar in place, and the programs of the church up and running, there is seldom need for a special board meeting. In these well-run churches, board meeting dates and times are in place for the year, and all business is cared for within this annual framework. These kinds of churches have a pastor who administers the business of the church within a small set of policies that define the outcomes already agreed upon by the pastor and the board.

More and more, well-administered churches find 12 monthly board business meetings more than they need. I know a fine church with a smooth administrative operation that meets for business every other month and uses the alternative meeting times for special projects, long-range planning, and church board education.

A very good friend of mine is the executive of a Fortune 500 company. He believes the Nazarene church boards he has served on in a variety of places where his corporation has moved him, all, have too many meetings for the amount of business they have assumed. In contrast, he cites his own company, which operates on four board meetings per year; and most of them last less than two hours. Most Nazarene institutions of higher education function well on two board meetings per year. And the General Board of the denomination meets annually.

As the Peter Principle says, people in a hierarchy tend to be promoted one level beyond their competence. Another law says a board will use all the time available on whatever is on the agenda regardless of whether it is consequential. My friend believes boards need to stay on the main line of prayerful planning and Spirit-filled leadership in the important decision-making areas, while they delegate most of what many boards put on their agendas. An increasing number of church boards are grasping this concept of more delegation and fewer meetings. Unfortunately, the smaller the church, the more likely it is to turn church administration over to the board and to see the pastor as their employee. Thus, the pastor is authorized, decision by decision, to administer the affairs of the church instead of being empowered to lead and manage.

There are several ways to enrich the purposes of 12 monthly church board meetings per year.

1. Use one meeting each quarter for church board education, including the possibility of a resource person coming in to discuss evangelism, teen challenges, family pressures, lay leadership, Holiness theology, or whatever else is appropriate for the board at the time. This can be enhanced as a dinner meeting with spouses.

2. Use an occasional meeting for prayer and sharing.

3. Take the church board to the district assembly.

4. Call a joint meeting of the outgoing and incoming board members at the junction of the old and new year for fellowship and open-ended discussion.

5. Use the December meeting as a Christmas gathering for all church board families. The Christmas season is a time for fellowship and bonding. Close the meeting with a devotional explanation by the pastor about the ministry

of the church board. As a vital resource for the next generation of lay leadership, the children who attend may get their first lessons in boardmanship.

6. Unless the idea offends the business sensibilities of the board's traditions, skip the August meeting in favor of a "time to catch our breath and begin again" with the opening of school.

There is, however, one word of warning. Never trivialize the work of the board or the importance of church board meetings. Boards who have done their planning well for the entire year can enrich their work with special meetings that increase their resources and bond them better to the church and to each other.

What Board Size Is Best?

The *Manual of the Church of the Nazarene* gives considerable latitude in the size of the church board. Besides the four ex officio members of the board—pastor, Sunday School superintendent, president of the Nazarene Youth International, and president of the Nazarene World Mission Society—the annual church meeting may elect from 3 to 13 stewards and from 3 to 9 trustees. This makes the total membership of the board no fewer than 10 and no more than 26.

Also, the church may choose to designate the Sunday School Ministries Board as the Education Committee of the church board, thus adding another three to nine elected persons to the board, plus the children's ministries director and the adult ministries director. (The pastor, NYI president, and NWMS president, who are ex officio members of the Sunday School Ministries Board, are already included on the board.) These adjustments would make possible a total church board membership of from 15 to 37 persons.

The possibility of an impractical board size in small congregations may be why the *Manual* provides that churches with 75 or fewer members may choose to have the church board assume the duties of the Sunday School Ministries Board.

However, the question is: *What is the best size for a church board?*

1. The church that is interested in the broadest possible representation of the congregation on the board may opt for the larger number of elected members. They believe that board is best that represents the greatest possible number of families in the church.

However, there is a downside to a large board:

• The large board is less flexible and more unwieldy for its sheer numbers. For instance, a large board cannot easily gather around a table. I was once interviewed by a church board with 37 members. The meeting looked like a small congregation, sitting in rows, looking around each other to see better.

• The larger board may include some persons who make a zero to minimal contribution to the decision-making process. A noncontributing member is likely to become a loose cannon when the pressure is on.

• The larger the board, the more work is done by committees. Only the very smallest and very largest decisions can be made well by a large group. Large groups do best in deciding to build a new church (big decision) or pay the electric bill (small decision). But the usual run of personnel and finance problems that clog the agendas of most boards are resolved best by small groups who include people with special skills and experience.

• The larger the board, the more likely it is to include one-issue members. Since every member on a large board cannot contribute to every discussion, members will select areas of greater personal concern for the focus of their influence.

2. There is also a downside to the smaller board.

• The small board has a constricted membership that is probably reelected year after year, thus developing a sense of ownership and need for control.

• There is less turnover and cross-congregational representation in a small board. Many people with much to contribute may not have an opportunity to serve.

3. Where is the point of balance in the size of a board?

• A cursory look at the ballot returns will probably show a number of laypersons who bunch up at the top with broad support from the greatest number in the congregation. These are the people to whom the congregation looks for leadership. These people need to be on the board because their influence counts with most people. In some churches this number may be no more than six, equal to three stewards and three trustees.

• Between the top vote-getters and those who also ran is usually a gap that sets the two groups apart in congregational leadership and influence. Someone needs to study these dynamics and determine how many of the latter group are needed to help make the board efficient without losing the important quality of representation.

• Larger churches tend to have smaller boards in relation to their membership, and thus less focus on representation and more focus on quality of lay leadership.

• One pastor I interviewed believes in a board small enough to ride in the church van to district meetings and seminars and big enough to gather around one configuration of four eight-foot tables formed in a square.

• The Nazarene *Manual* is silent on the question of an advisory council that meets on occasion with the pastor and the board. Most churches would profit by a quarterly or semiannual meeting of all the church workers, including the volunteers who work in Sunday School, the musicians, the ushers, the greeters, and others. Some churches broaden this meeting to include all those who contribute systematically to the church.

Christian colleges who use this advisory council idea usually have an annual recognition dinner highlighting the work of the donors and volunteers, giving them an update on institutional affairs and a time for questions and answers. These occasions could offer the pastor a great opportunity for showcasing his or her vision. If this approach would help more people feel they were a part of what is going on, it is worth the try.

What Are the Best Arrangements?

I only wish every church could afford a designated boardroom with ample space for doing their work and comfortable furnishings worthy of the contribution of the church board to the church.

The boardroom need not be reserved for the exclusive use of the board but rather assigned for the purposes that dignify its existence, such as staff meetings, committee meetings, and an adult Sunday School class. It is even possible that some mature or older adult would provide funds for furnishing the room in honor of a historic family or beloved lay leader in the church.

But whether or not the church has vision for a boardroom, the circumstances of the actual board meetings are of no small importance. Let's assume the ideal setting and then settle for what our vision affords.

1. The worst setting is a head table for the pastor with the board members seated in rows like a jury ready to vote thumbs up or thumbs down. This structures the

discussions to center on the pastor, making it harder for remarks to be addressed to each other.

2. Most boat-shaped conference tables are built for 10 or 12 people and are ideal for smaller boards. Beautiful used conference tables are available. The most attractive table I ever saw was in a Salvation Army thrift store, a left-over item from an estate sale. Some churches have crafts-men in their congregations who can make a handsome table for the church board, thus increasing its emotional value to the congregation.

3. The larger board, according to the shape of their room, can configure eight-foot banquet tables in a square or oblong shape for the comfort of the board. Green felt tablecloths improve the looks of the tables and serve as modesty panels. The tables may be decorated or plain. Some boards have candy dishes, pitchers of water, and drinking glasses on the tables. To keep everyone from sit-ting in the same place each month, some boards use name cards, which are reassigned for each meeting.

4. A carpeted floor not only looks good but also re-duces the sounds of scraping feet.

5. In this day of the media highway, videos, projec-tors, slides, flip charts, and chalkboards, every boardroom needs media equipment. Hardware and software are go-ing to be common tools in the future of effective boards.

6. Some large churches serve a meal at every church board meeting so meeting times can be set earlier and more opportunity may be available for informal conversa-tion and bonding. Even churches who resist the idea may find that refreshments—cookies and coffee—are useful means for encouraging fellowship and breaking up the meetings into segments. Some boards serve refreshments during a break when board committees meet.

7. For the pure purpose of beauty, a Paul Revere chan-

delier above the board table may be worth what it costs.

8. In this day of high-tech office equipment, the agenda and all reports will be more useful if they have been word processed and hard copies are made available to all members. If the church publishes a midweek paper, it may include a monthly spot titled "Church Board News and Information." People like to feel they are informed.

9. A handsome cabinet will add style to the boardroom and will serve as a place to save and display artifacts of the church that symbolize parts of its history. This may be the place to keep the official record books that document memberships, baptisms, weddings, deaths, and the like. Nearly every church that has gone through a building program and/or a local change has items that should be preserved in the boardroom.

10. Heating and cooling systems need to meet two standards: adequate capacity and quietness. Johnny Carson insisted on keeping the temperature in the studio of his late-night television show at 66 degrees because this is, according to him, the breakpoint between being too cold or too warm. People who feel cold are irritated; people who feel too warm are lethargic.

11. There is one more item that is not related to the development of the boardroom but is important to church board arrangements: Most board members will keep themselves better organized and informed if they are given a notebook at the beginning of the year for all their church board information. These notebooks are available at wholesale, commercial supply houses for minimal costs and may include the name of each board member embossed on the cover. The notebook may include space for the following:

• Roster of pastoral staff and volunteers, including phone numbers.

• Roster of church board membership, with addresses, phone numbers, birthdays, and anniversaries.

• Church organizational charts, including the auxiliaries, Sunday School, NYI, and NWMS.

• The official calendar for the year. There can be only one official calendar, which should include all events for the year and be updated monthly for the board.

• A vision sheet with goals, priorities, and anticipated church program results for the current year. Expected results from each church program need to be always in the minds of the church board members.

• Annual audit and departmental reports.

• Annual budget with comparative figures for the last three years.

• Monthly dividers for holding current minutes, treasurer's report, pastor's report, committee reports, and other pertinent data.

• District minutes in the side pocket.

A closing word: Not every board will see a need to do all the things suggested in this chapter on the advantages of good board arrangements. However, it is hoped these suggestions will heighten awareness of the importance of detailed preparation for board meetings in all churches where the work of the pastor and the board are considered to be vitally important.

4

Robert's Rules
and Other Kinds of Order

 The purpose of this chapter is to explain the rules and procedures necessary for good board meetings.

IN THE OLD TESTAMENT there is no evidence of business meetings that called on people to make motions, pass resolutions, or even think about church business as we do.

In the New Testament, the Church in Jerusalem chose Matthias to take the place of Judas. But they made their decision between two candidates by casting lots (Acts 1:15-26).

When the Jerusalem Church faced the murmuring Grecian Jews, who said the widows of their group were being neglected, the apostles asked the people to choose seven Spirit-filled men with good reputations for honesty and wisdom whom the apostles would "appoint over this business" (Acts 6:3, NKJV). Apparently the church nominated their candidates, and the apostles officially appointed them (vv. 1-7).

During the big Jerusalem conference on grace and law, there were no motions and amendments. But "the apostles and elders, with the whole church, decided" (Acts 15:22), and what they decided "seemed good to the Holy Spirit and to us" (v. 28). The Jerusalem conference met their theological challenge by consensus without motions and resolutions.

The Need for Rules of Order

The 20th-century Church has come a long way from the winding cobblestone streets of Jerusalem. The house church of the New Testament era has been replaced by well-organized congregations. Many of these well-administered churches find their identity within the bureaucratic structures of a denomination. Churches are chartered as not-for-profit corporations.

In most states the law requires the church, as a corporation, to provide a board of trustees who are charged with certain responsibilities for the congregation's property and financing. Almost all churches of size administrate themselves as corporate models. In the larger churches, pastors are sometimes described as CEOs who preach on Sundays.

While the church was developing its corporate organizational model, a corollary in parliamentary procedure was finding root in rules of order that are now taken for granted in most board meetings and congregational business sessions.

In 1876 Maj. Henry M. Robert, a United States Army engineer, was asked to chair business meetings in his own church. Sensing the need for rules of order that would make the democratic decision-making process fair and efficient, he went home one night to set about writing what is now the widely accepted *Robert's Rules of Order.*

There is a statement near the conclusion of the Special Rules in the *Manual of the Church of the Nazarene* that confirms for Nazarenes what most other organizations also follow in parliamentary procedure: "The meetings and proceedings of the members of the Church of the Nazarene, local, district, and general, and the committees of the corporation shall be regulated and controlled according to *Robert's Rules of Order* (latest edition) for parliamentary procedure" (40).

Three Megaqualities of Boards in Churches

Unless the members of the church board understand and follow the rules, a meeting can become confused and even get out of hand. Before discussing how to run a board meeting, every church board needs to understand the three megaqualities for doing business in the name of Christ. The meeting must be (1) democratic, (2) efficient, and (3) Christian.

No church board meeting is *democratic* unless every member is given an opportunity—even urged—to express his or her opinion on the concerns and be listened to seriously. Poor manners, such as yelling, interrupting the other person while he or she is trying to express an idea, or putting someone down with loud rejections of his or her idea or opinion, fall short of the Christian ideal in decision making. A church board process dominated by one unmannerly person who intimidates others is sick, and prayer needs to be offered for its healing.

A church board decision-making process is *efficient* when the group disciplines itself to stay with the matter at hand, allowing everyone to speak fully, answering all questions adequately, and then deciding the issue by a majority vote. The majority vote is then supported by the entire board.

To be *Christian,* a church board meeting needs (1) the absence of some things and (2) the presence of others.

No board meeting is Christian when the discussion becomes harsh, angry, hurtful, punitive, judgmental, or embarrassingly personal. The Spirit of Christ is not compatible with bursts of verbal abuse, finger-pointing, or slammed doors. Christians seeking God's will for His church do not walk out of meetings. The only apostle who walked out on a meeting was Judas. The slightest suggestion of physical abuse is totally off-limits in the deliberations of a church board. Christians do not talk to each other with clenched fists. They listen to each other with open hearts.

A church board meeting is Christian when mutual respect and acceptance are reflected in all relationships. It is Christian to accept the person without condoning his or her unacceptable behavior. Even when a woman was caught in adultery, Jesus did not castigate her. He called for any of her accusers who were without sin to step forward. When all the lecherous men had turned away, Jesus said, "Neither do I condemn thee: go, and sin no more" (John 8:11, KJV).

If Jesus served on a modern church board, He would love the thoughtless teens who vandalized the church van on their last trip—without condoning what they did. He would use the occasion of their unacceptable behavior to teach responsibility, not to alienate them from himself. At least that is how Jesus dealt with Peter, who got out of hand when he "began to curse and to swear, saying, I know not this man of whom ye speak" (Mark 14:71, KJV).

Instead of calling Peter before a disciplinary panel, Jesus met him at a campfire built at a familiar spot on the shore of their beloved lake. Forgiveness and reconciliation became reality in a man-to-man talk in a relaxed atmosphere where no fingers were pointed nor voices raised. And the cursing fisherman became the Spirit-filled preacher on Pentecost Sunday.

There is an important footnote to the story of Peter's rise from denying Christ in the courtyard to preaching the sermon on Pentecost Sunday. Peter could not have been the leader of Christ's Church in Jerusalem if the apostles had not been willing to open their arms and hearts to a brother whose feet of clay were highly visible.

The apostles did not constitute a church board. However, they had in their close-knit group the power to freeze out Peter if they had chosen. But they were Christian in their willingness to follow God-called leadership without getting hung up over human failure. May God apply the lesson in places where the pastor's feet of clay have become the occasion of stumbling among people who have higher standards for others than they sometimes do for themselves.

Order in the Meeting

A church board meeting officially begins when the pastor calls it to order. If a quorum is present—at least half of the members—the board is ready to do business. The board now has authority to address matters wherein its responsibility lies.

No member has authority outside a session of the board unless that authority has been assigned specifically by the board. In other words, board members as persons do not have authority to tell the pastor, staff, and volunteers what to do or to make commitments in the name of the church. That authority stays within the board.

Lay board members with tendencies to boss church personnel or make commitments in the name of the church need to be reminded of their limitations. And personnel who have been put upon by church board members, acting on their own authority, need to be protected by the board.

Following the call to order, several things happen sequentially:

• Time is taken for reading the Scriptures, praying, and listening to a devotional thought.

Different laypersons—one for each monthly meeting—can be assigned the devotional period. If the service of the church board is a ministry, and I believe it is, then sharing and praying together are more than appropriate—they are a priority. A spiritual opening sets the tone for the rest of the meeting.

• The first item of business is the roll call.

"Regrets" that have been received from those who are unable to attend are recorded. Minutes on the roll call should include the names of all board members, those who are present and those who are not. There may be an occasion in the future when this attendance record is very important.

• Now comes the reading of the minutes from the last meeting.

Opportunity is made for corrections, omissions, additions, or explanations. Some boards lose *past motions* that were acted upon but have not been fulfilled. Unfulfilled motions passed by the board in previous meetings need to be kept alive by carrying them forward. Motions that have been fulfilled may deserve a word of explanation or report. Dealing with the minutes of the board is an important matter.

Besides reading the minutes, the secretary needs to report on any congregational *membership changes*, including deaths, transfers, new members by letter, new members by profession of faith, and current total membership. If membership is as important as many say it is, the church board needs to be kept apprised of its status.

The secretary may report on *correspondence* received or sent in the name of the church board. Copies of this correspondence need to be filed with the church board minutes. This is the place in the meeting when correspondence from the district office may be reported. Otherwise, it dies on the desk of the secretary or pastor.

The next block of business by the board is to hear whatever reports the board feels are appropriate.

In many well-organized churches, these reports include those from (1) the pastor, (2) the NYI president, (3) the NWMS president, (4) the Sunday School superintendent, and (5) monthly or quarterly reports from staff members.

These reports to the board should be word-processed and rarely more than one page in length, except for the report of the pastor, who should have whatever time he or she feels is necessary for written remarks to the board. These reports need to be filed with the minutes of the meeting in which they were given and preserved in the notebooks of the board members.

• The centerpiece of most church board meetings—going all the way back to Dr. Bresee's board meetings—is the *financial report.* In most small churches this report comes from the treasurer. In some church organizations the treasurer reports to the financial secretary, who makes the report to the board. I know of churches who receive the financial report from the chairman of the Finance Committee. This is a matter of board preference and organization.

In any case, the monthly financial report must be hard copy, with columns that relate the month's figures to (1) the annual budget year-to-date figure, (2) last month's figures, and (3) figures from the same month a year ago. No numbers are useful unless they are placed in relation to other numbers that give them significance.

It is a personal matter, but I have insisted on a *financial report in prose,* which forces the writer to interpret the numbers for everyone, especially those who are not accustomed to reading balance sheets and year-to-date financial sheets. Numbers are only symbols, which can become confusing in their raw state. If the board does insist on a report in prose, the numbers sheets become backup for questions and detail.

Next on the agenda come the new and old concerns for discussion.

If the board functions as *a committee of the whole* and all business is brought before the entire board for discussion, this is the place in the agenda where old or new matters of concern are brought before the board. If these concerns come in the form of recommendations, they should be in writing with the upside and downside explained for each recommendation.

The church board can discuss a concern at length before a motion is finally made that hopefully is based on the consensus of the group. Otherwise, a motion made at the time of the recommendation forces the board to vote it up or down and to possibly divide the group with amendments or substitute motions.

If the board functions with *standing committees,* this is the place in the agenda in which matters of concern are brought up by members of the board, and references are made to the various committees who research, study, and discuss the matter until they are ready to bring back a recommendation to the board.

The committee recommendation, when it is brought, should follow this pattern: There needs to be (1) a full clarification of the problem or need; (2) three or more possible ways to meet the need, with reasons for and against each reason; and (3) the recommendation the committee feels is best and the reason why. The final decision belongs to the church board, not to the committee, unless the committee was given power to act.

• At this point, some boards break for brief committee meetings, which are often long enough to thrash out small matters.

However, each committee should expect to hold a separate meeting during the month if their business load warrants it. Some boards also serve coffee and cookies or dessert at this time. These refreshment duties may be assigned, or volunteered for by a board member and his or her spouse, for each regular meeting during the year. Boards who do not function with standing committees may simply have a refreshments break at this time if they desire.

Following the refreshments break, the reports of the standing committees and the special committees are heard.

The board may vote to (1) *receive* a report, in which case it is filed without action; (2) *adopt* a report, which includes its recommendations; or (3) receive a report and adopt its recommendations *seriatim* (individually).

Next comes the closing segment of the meeting.

Any further business may include (1) announcements, (2) additional references, or (3) matters of personal privilege. The meeting is adjourned by a prayer of benediction.

Minutes, Motions, and Committees

Board members need to be serious about the keeping of minutes by an efficient, conscientious person who is the elected secretary.

Keeping the minutes

There is no need for secretaries to summarize discussion, because summaries of what people have said cannot be fully accurate. The plainest kind of minutes is a numbered succession of business actions by the board, from one to infinity. This numerical system makes it possible for the board to refer to any one item of business by number so all will quickly and fully understand the point of question or discussion. But regardless of the system used, the minutes must be accurate.

Because of the litigious society we live in, many boards have stopped identifying the name of the persons who made the motion and second. Indemnification at the price of an insurance policy is looking much more like a necessity than a luxury to an increasing number of boards these days.

Minutes need to be kept in an official binder that can be expanded to several inches thick as necessary. This volume is a handy reference tool for times to come. Some boards keep double sets of binderies. In this day of word processing, floppy disks or other computer devices may be used for keeping additional sets of minutes in a vault or strongbox. Fire and theft are unpleasant possibilities.

Some boards are willing for the minutes to be dormant until they are read at the next monthly meeting. Other boards want their minutes distributed by mail within 10 days after each meeting so members may refresh themselves on their responsibilities.

Making a motion

Church board minutes are important because they contain the record of motions acted on by the board. *A motion is a brief, precise statement of a proposed action.*

• No member can make a motion until he or she has been recognized—given permission to speak—by the chairman, who is the pastor.

• No motion can be discussed until it has been seconded by a member of the board.

The person who makes a second thereby gives his or her support to the motion. This procedure keeps the group from spending time on some matter that is the concern of only one person.

• Discussion follows the clarification of the motion. If there is need, the chairman calls for the secretary to read the motion so all minds are clear.

• The board may do several things with a motion under discussion. (1) It can be *passed* as stated. (2) It may be *amended* by a vote of the board. If so, the amended motion must then be stated and discussed as amended. (3) The motion may be *tabled* for future reference. Or the motion may be *tabled indefinitely,* which means the motion is dead. (4) The motion may be *referred* to a committee for further study and a report back to the board.

The vote

• *When to vote.* After everyone who desires to speak has spoken, or after the board has voted to end discussion by a two-thirds vote, the chairman usually calls for the motion to be read again before a vote is called.

• *Kinds of votes.* The chairman may call for a *voice* vote: those for and those against. Or he or she may call for *hands* to be raised. If the pastor or a board member is not sure the voice vote was decisive, a hand vote may be called for. Any member may call for a *ballot* vote, and the request must be honored. The pastor is a voting member of the board.

• *Elections.* Most motions and elections of board officers are decided by plurality—the most votes. However, a two-thirds vote is needed (1) to *suspend* the rules or (2) to *end debate.* The board may nominate a new pastor by a majority vote, but it takes a two-thirds majority of the congregation vote to elect him or her.

The Pros and Cons of Committees

There are two kinds of church board committees. (1) Some boards have standing committees, which function throughout the church year dealing with whatever business the board refers to them. (2) Then there are special committees—ad hoc—that are appointed, usually by the pastor on action by the board. Those ad hoc committees deal with a specific matter assigned them by the board. When their assignment is completed and they have reported back to the board, the committee ceases to exist.

The most common church board organization that uses standing committees includes the following.

The Finance Committee develops the budget, monitors the church finances, expands congregational stewardship, supervises purchasing with business procedures, and approves expenditures over a predetermined amount that the committee feels might upset the current financial condition of the church, even though the funds are budgeted.

The danger in a strong finance committee is that they may become a board within the board—even a veto squad. The advantage in a good finance committee is the maintenance of balance between income and expenditure. Unfunded projects are destructive to the regular financing of the church. Sometimes the money people give to special projects comes from their regular giving. Thus, the project is paid for, but the operating budget suffers. It is better to raise all project money after the regular operating budget is in hand.

The Business and Property Committee supervises the maintenance and cleaning of the property and cares for church-owned vehicles, parking lots, shrubbery, and decorating.

It is important that this committee assures that funds for its work are in the annual budget as line items. It should not need to fight for dollars on a crisis-by-crisis basis. Some church boards have inadvertently shifted their maintenance dollars into other areas such as expanded staff and then do not have adequate budget for proper maintenance of their property.

The Program and Planning Committee sets or recommends policies for the operation of the church office, kitchen, visitation program, church calendar, advertising and printing, music, Communion, special events, and evangelism. People with enthusiasm and vision are needed on this committee. Much of their work is creative and behind the scenes, but it is very important. Their work often requires considerable follow-through.

Christian education, missionary projects, and youth work come under the aegis of the Sunday School superintendent, NWMS president, NYI president, and their official councils and committees. However, the church board needs to be apprised of the work of these auxiliaries and should feel free to give input as needed.

The Pastor and Parish Committee consists of the chairmen of the three standing committees. They meet informally with the pastor to discuss relationships with the pastor and various constituencies within the church, the pastor's personal concerns, and other matters of mutual interest.

This committee keeps no minutes and makes no reports. It is strictly advisory as a relationship-building group. This is the group who knows when and why the pastor is away. His or her vacation time is a matter of policy, but when it is to be taken may be a matter of good timing at home. The pastor and the church's Pastor and Parish Committee need to stay in touch.

The biggest single hurdle to developing a committee system within the church board is the natural fear of some pastors who think the release of their authority over all that happens will diminish their leadership. However, once laypersons are convinced the pastor means business in allowing them to make decisions and give leadership to *the secular side of the church operation,* it is amazing how they will develop into supportive leaders. As in Acts 6, the pastor will be more free to serve as spiritual leader when laypersons feel fulfilled in substantive responsibilities by a proper division of labor.

Terms You Need to Know

The following terms do not constitute a lexicon. The list is incomplete and informal. However, they are a good place to start for those who want to understand the common vocabulary of boards.

Adjourn: to end the meeting.

Agenda: the list of matters for consideration.

Amendment: a change made in a motion.

Chairman pro tempore: the temporary chairman.

Division of the house: a count of votes by show of hands.

Majority: one more than half of those voting.

Pending question: any motion open for discussion.

Personal privilege: the request of a board member to speak on a matter unrelated to the agenda. It is often used to express appreciation or call a matter to the attention of the group.

Plurality: the largest number of votes received in an election of three or more persons.

Point of order: an objection raised because of possible improper procedure.

Previous question: a motion to end debate and vote immediately. Needs a two-thirds majority to carry.

Quorum: the number necessary to do business, usually half of the membership.

Ratify: to approve some action already taken, such as an action by the chairman.

Recess: a temporary break in the meeting, such as for refreshments.

Unanimous consent: a request by the chairman in which differences of opinion are not expected. It is sometimes used in correcting minutes or even approving them.

The Five Main Motions

• Introduce business: "I move . . ." is debatable. Takes a majority vote.

• Take up a matter previously tabled: "I move we take from the table . . ." is not debatable. Takes a majority vote.

• Reconsider a matter already voted: "I move we reconsider our action to . . ." is debatable. Takes a majority vote.

• Strike out a motion already disposed of: "I move we rescind the action already passed on . . ." is debatable. Takes a majority vote.

• Consider a matter out of its scheduled order: "I move we suspend the rules and consider . . ." is not debatable. Takes a two-thirds vote.

Not every detail of rule and protocol can or should be covered in this overview. However, most boards do their best work in a relaxed atmosphere in which consensus reigns over rules of order. Rules of order render their best service when there is confusion and the proper procedure must be applied. Above all, good manners and Christlike attitudes are the hallmarks of good church board meetings.

5

How Pastors and Board Members Are Alike but Different

 The purpose of this chapter is to summarize a research report on the qualities and views of pastors and laypersons on the board.

THERE ARE MORE THAN 50,000 Nazarene members serving on local church boards in North America. In addition to the elected lay representatives, each board also includes three ex officio members: the Sunday School superintendent, the local Nazarene World Mission Society president, and the Nazarene Youth International president. Taken together, these people constitute the single most important official group in any local church.

Until now, no attempt has been made to determine what kinds of people congregations choose for this important assignment, nor how their personal qualities and views compare and contrast with their pastor, who, by *Manual* authority, serves as chairman of the board.

Under the sponsorship of the Church Growth Division, a study has been made that for the first time identifies who gets elected to the board. The focus in this chapter will be on the results of that study.

Although any attempt to identify the traits of church board members must allow for individual variations of some magnitude, there is such a thing, statistically, as the typical Nazarene church board member. The typical board member is one who exhibits more of the qualities and characteristics shared among board members than others do. To put it another way, the typical Nazarene board member has a majority of the characteristics shared by most members of the board denomination-wide.

What are the typical characteristics of church board members?

To begin with, there are some significant social gaps among persons serving on the board.

• The majority of lay board members are men (55%), and almost all pastors (97%) are male.

• Only 4% of the lay board members are non-Caucasian, and even fewer (3%) of the pastors are non-Caucasian.

• Although most of the lay board members (69%) and pastors (79%) are between the ages of 35 and 64, 18% of the lay board members are 65 or older, while a mere 6% of the pastors are of retirement age. Apparently board members stay on while pastors retire.

As might be expected, lay board members are financially more secure than their pastors.

• Over half of the laypersons (51%) do not have children living at home, while a smaller proportion (35%) of the pastors and spouses have an empty nest.

• A significant proportion of laypersons (85%) are buying their homes, and 36% have their homes paid for.

• In spite of the home-buying trend that started for pastors in the 1960s, because of tax considerations most pastors still live in parsonages.

Pastors have more formal education than board members.

• More than half (52%) of the pastors have attended

graduate school, and 32% more (a total of 84%) have graduated from college, while 34% of laypersons have not gone beyond high school, and only 19% have graduated from college. This means that most younger pastors are paying off college and seminary debts for more than a decade into their ministry, when income is usually in short supply.

• However, in spite of their years of advanced formal education, more than half of the pastors (56%) make less than $24,000 annually. Forty-four percent of the laypersons earn between $25,000 and $49,000, contrasted to 37% of the pastors. There are 18% of the laypersons and only 7% of the pastors in the annual income bracket above $50,000.

• As for employment, 37% of the lay board members are hourly workers, 23% salaried, and 20% self-employed; 10% of the women identify themselves as homemakers.

• A total of 34% of the lay board members report they are in management, 31% say they do office work, and 22% are in the professions, while 17% work in factories. Only 8% of the board members work in agriculture.

Pastors have a long, strong denominational connection.

• More than half (53%) of the pastors are second- or third-generation Nazarenes. Almost three-fourths of the pastors (74%) have been members of the Church of the Nazarene for more than 20 years. However, 85% have been in their present pastorate for fewer than 9 years.

• Laypersons, on the other hand, are less likely (42%) to come from second- and third-generation Nazarene families. They have been Nazarenes for fewer years (39% under 20 years), and 42% have been members of their local Nazarene church for 9 years or less. These numbers must indicate the churches are gaining new members from outside the Nazarene corral.

The Typical Nazarene Board Member

The typical layperson on the church board is a married man in his productive years who has been a Nazarene for more than 20 years. He works in an office and lives with his wife in their own home on a middle-class income. Either their family is raised, or their teens will soon be young adults. He has a high school diploma and probably attended college. Besides serving on the board, this layperson either teaches a Sunday School class, sings in the choir, or serves as an usher.

The Typical Nazarene Pastor

The typical pastor in the Church of the Nazarene is a man who lives in a parsonage with his wife on an annual income of $15,000 to $34,000. Besides holding a college diploma, he probably has a graduate degree as well, most likely from Nazarene Theological Seminary. His family tends to be younger and larger than families of board members. He is well-educated, underpaid, idealistic, and a hard worker.

How do board members feel about their church?

Pastors and laypersons agree on the condition of the church.

• A third of the board members feel their church is growing, 28% believe it is beginning to grow, another 28% believe the church is stalemated, and 11% see their church declining.

When it comes to identifying the main factor in growth or no growth, the pastors and lay board members have the same priorities.

• Pastors and laypersons see the most important growth factor as the spiritual condition of the church (lay 42% and pastors 38%).

• Next in importance is the work of the congregation (lay 25% and pastors 35%).

• Third is the pastor and staff (lay 23% and pastors 15%).

• Fourth is church location and building facility (lay 9% and pastors 7%).

• And finally, at the bottom of the list of important growth factors, is the church board (lay 2% and pastors 6%).

Apparently few people understand the real purpose of the board, which is to represent the congregation in working with the pastor in (1) clarifying the vision of the church, (2) identifying the results they plan to achieve, (3) organizing the church to achieve their desired results, and (4) providing the positive atmosphere necessary for growth and development.

• More than half (52%) of the churches make the board minutes available to the congregation. However, a policy manual is lacking in 65% of the churches.

Apparently, a significant proportion of the churches function with a fairly high level of unity.

• More than two-thirds of the lay board members (72%) and pastors (68%) say they usually have unity on the board.

• Approximately the same proportion (72% and 75% respectively) are usually encouraged at the end of the monthly meeting.

• Only 7% of the lay board members and pastors feel frustrated by the board meetings.

There is a split decision on whether the board is dominated by one strong family.

• Twenty-one percent of the laypersons say they feel they are dominated by one strong family, while 34% of the pastors say they believe they are.

• However, only 28% of the lay board members and 31% of the pastors say they believe the influence of the leading family is negative. This is in contrast to the widely held view that the influence of a dominant family on the church board spells trouble.

When asked about their one wish or prayer for their church, the lay board members and the pastors did not see things alike.

• The number one concern (40%) of the pastors was for more vision for the future, while the laypersons were almost equally split on more vision for the future (30%) and more money (29%).

• The second concern for the pastors (28%) was for more spiritual leadership.

There was uncertainty among the lay board members and the pastors about the purpose of the church board.

• The number one purpose of the board, as seen by both the laypersons (98%) and the pastors (96%), is "to work with the pastor."

• However, a surprising number of lay board members (57%) and pastors (45%) believe the purpose of the board is "to run the church."

• The idea of the board as a watchdog on what the pastor does was resisted strongly by the laypersons (80%) and even more strongly by pastors (89%).

When asked to identify the biggest challenges faced by the church board, pastors and lay board members agreed:

• The most important challenge of the church board is "the spiritual tide of the church" (lay 86% and pastors 96%).

• The second most important challenge is "the education of the next generation" (lay 65% and pastors 66%).

• When the "biggest challenge" question was put in a negative form to test reliability, the results were the same.

How does the church board feel about budgets and finances?

• When asked about the Nazarene budget system, 38% of the board members said, "The system is fair," and another 37% said it is "acceptable." Only 13% said, "The system is unfair."

• More than two-thirds of the laypersons (68%) said, "I have a pretty good idea how the budget money is spent." Not surprisingly, more pastors (81%) feel they know where the money goes.

• However, another 27% of the laypersons and 17% of the pastors said, "I'm not up on how the money is spent, but I'd like to know."

• On the mention of money from the pulpit, 38% of the board thought money was talked about too often. Maybe that is because 94% of the board members say they tithe.

• Nearly a third (31%) of the board members say the budget money is the hardest to raise, followed by 27% who say they believe "it is just hard to pay the local bills."

Most churches have a mortgage.

• At the time of this study, 29% of the church boards had church construction under way, and another 35% said they had completed a building program in the last five years.

• A whopping 72% of the churches are mortgaged, and 39% of the boards say their mortgage is a burden.

• When it comes to a professional staff, nearly half (49%) of the churches have no staff.

• Of those churches who do have staff, however, 47% of the board members say they believe their expenditure for professional staff is about right or should be increased. It seems that having a professional staff to extend the ministry of the church is here to stay and is on the increase.

What denominational awareness do church board members have?

• Only 34% of the board members were delegates to their last district assembly.

• However, the board members did better by the General Assembly, since 45% were delegates or visitors to the last one.

• Around 64% of the board members know the name of the general superintendent who chaired their last district assembly or is currently in jurisdiction.

• When it comes to the regional Nazarene college or university, 54% of the board members know the name of the president.

• Only 25% of the board members believe Nazarene affiliation is "the most important factor in choosing a college," while 31% are apparently open to sending Nazarene students to any college with a Christian philosophy.

• As in the general population, "proximity to home" is the most important factor in choosing a college, even among Nazarene church board members (75%) and pastors (50%).

A Tribute to Nazarene Church Board Members

Some persons spoof board members, saying they should be buried 10 feet in the ground—because "down deep" they are good people. But board members in the Church of the Nazarene *are* good people. Many small churches on hard times have been kept alive by the loyalty and sacrificial giving of board members who asked very little in return.

In some churches, boards have held things together when the congregation was about to blow apart—particularly in smaller churches, where board members have seen pastors come and go far too often. They have helped move the new pastor in with a feeling of anticipation. And very often, after too short a tenure, they helped the pastor's family pack their belongings and then have waved good-bye to one more truck that left the disappointments of the church board behind.

Faithful church members have dealt with crises of all sorts, including heartrending pastor breakdowns and congregational conflicts out of control. But when the dust cleared and the storm passed, these board members were right where they had always been: praying around the altar, singing, testifying, paying the bills, and ready to support yet another pastor.

Out of sheer commitment, some board members have paid the budgets rather than attend the district assembly and feel embarrassed. They have cooperated by voting for expansions they were finally left to pay off when the original enthusiasm waned.

If some board members occasionally feel put upon and respond in kind, it is not because they are carnal. It is because they are human, just like the rest of us. They deserve our love and appreciation. And we should not wait until they are 6 or 10 feet down under before we express it. A Church Board Appreciation Day might be a warmhearted idea for your church.

A Theology for Board Members and Other Nazarenes

 The purpose of this chapter is to relate the theology of Nazarenes.

EVERY BOARD MEMBER NEEDS to take seriously the admonition of Peter:

> *Sanctify the Lord God in your hearts:*
> *and be ready always to give an answer to every man*
> *that asketh you a reason*
> *of the hope that is in you*
> *with meekness and fear.*
> —1 Pet. 3:15, KJV

Peter could not have made this statement about "a reason of the hope that is in you" during the earlier years of his fishing career on Galilee. He was flawed by an inordinate desire to be approved. He made promises he could not keep, pledges he could not pay, talked when he should have been listening, attempted the impossible, denied to a slave girl that he even knew Jesus, and then swore to make his point. By modern standards, Peter was in no position to talk with anybody about what beliefs they lived by.

God used Simon Peter to preach the sermon at Pentecost in spite of the flaws in his personality. It might be said that Peter preached in the service that changed his life forever. He grew in the faith *following* Pentecost, not before it. His immaturity gave way to Christian understanding, and his stature among the early Christians had the hallmarks of religious statesmanship.

Peter, who had never seen or heard of a church board, focused on the very heart of boardmanship when he said in essence: *Know God in your heart. And know why you believe what you believe.* This is the personal standard of faith and practice for every Nazarene church board member.

Although the *Manual* of the church includes all the *Articles of Faith* and an *Agreed Statement of Belief* for new church members, there is an irreducible minimum of theological understanding every layperson needs to bring to his or her service on the board. It is unconscionable to think of a church board member who does not possess deep convictions on the fundamental beliefs of Christian doctrine and living.

Each of our characters is shaped by what we really believe down deep. Everyone has notions about life. But in the mind of all persons are a few steadfast beliefs they are willing to stake their lives on.

For instance, I have a *notion* that, within limits, the power of positive thinking works. However, I have a *conviction* based on a steadfast belief in the resurrection of Christ, that my sins are forgiven, and that my name is recorded in the book of heaven. There is a great difference between a notion and a conviction, and it is tragic when these are mixed.

An Irreducible Minimum

Christian faith consists of only a few convictions that have their source in the Scriptures. What board members believe about the (1) authority, (2) inspiration, and (3) infallibility of the Scriptures determines whether their theology consists of notions collected in bits and pieces or whether their faith rests on a set of bedrock beliefs that attend the soul and illumine the values of life. What church board members believe about the Bible determines what they believe about Christ, sin, salvation, Christian living, and the events around the Last Judgment.

As the crown of God's creation, man is possessed of a special mark the Bible calls "the image of God." But man's life fails to conform to this image naturally and is, in its failed condition, bent away from God. This conflict between man as he was intended to be and man as he is cannot be resolved by intellectual or moral striving alone.

Alienated from his own being, man has violated God's law and is subject to the law of sin and death. To become what he was intended to be, man needs the grace of God to break the power of sin and let him be reborn. God provided the means for this grace in the incarnation of Jesus Christ.

Christ the Son and the Holy Spirit were equal with God the Father and were with God from the beginning. These three—Father, Son, and Holy Spirit—constitute the Trinity, which is one in "essence" but three in "Persons."

The walk of Christ on earth was God's way of demonstrating what life could be like. The kingdom of God, as Jesus preached it, was the reign of God in the lives of persons who accepted His Lordship. Christ's death and resurrection marked the end of the law of sin and death for all who believed in Him as God's Son and received His grace.

The absolute, irreducible, minimum expression of Christian faith is (1) unquestioned belief in the incarnation of God in Christ, (2) His sinless life, (3) His death, which bore in it the suffering for the sins of everyone, and (4) the power of His resurrection, which sets all sinners free from the law of sin and death. The Holy Spirit, who inspired those who wrote the Scriptures, nurtures the Church as the Body of Christ on earth today. And finally, the consummation of the divine plan for salvation will come at the end of history with the resurrection of the dead and the appearance of Jesus Christ as the Judge of all mankind.

Until then, the role of the church board is to join hands with the pastor and the congregation in (1) celebrating the Church's hope, (2) nurturing its people, and (3) reaching out to those whose beliefs have not brought them eternal life.

Nazarene Theology

Although Nazarene board members do not need to be professional theologians, they do need to know what the church believes.

The 16 Articles of Faith and the 8 statements in the Agreed Statement of Belief can be discussed in roundtable groups or may be presented in a study session by the pastor or another capable theologian. But Nazarene board members, above all others in the church, need to have their questions on theology answered. Only then can they "give an answer to every man" who asks "a reason of the hope that is in" them.

Warmhearted, professional, Nazarene theologians who teach primarily in colleges, universities, and seminaries can expound, explain, and debate the fine points of theology with a language all their own. They are good men and women to be cherished by the church. But professional theological writings are not always easily understood by ordinary suburban Christians.

Harriet Beecher Stowe's grandfather was a blacksmith in Connecticut in the days when American blacksmiths had their own libraries and read from them regularly. It is no wonder that a Yale pundit said Lyman Beecher was the father of more brains than any man in America. Not many laypersons today read theology regularly from the books of professional theologians. But that does not mean they are not interested in theology, nor does it mean they do not know what they believe. However, most laypersons need their theology expressed in plain talk.

In lay terms, every board member needs to know the theology of the church. It is the job of the pastor, as resident theologian and teacher, to lead the church board in understanding that theology. The *Manual* provides Nazarenes with the (1) the course of study outline, (2) accurate summary statements, (3) and Scripture references for the following theological beliefs of the church:

I. The Triune God
    We believe in one eternally existent, infinite God, Sovereign of the universe; . . . that He, as God, is Triune in essential being, revealed as Father, Son, and Holy Spirit. . . .

II. Jesus Christ
    We believe in Jesus Christ . . . that He became incarnate by the Holy Spirit and was born of the Virgin Mary, so that two whole and perfect natures . . . are thus united in one Person very God and very man, the God-man. . . .

III. The Holy Spirit
    We believe in the Holy Spirit . . . that He is ever present and efficiently active in and with the Church . . .

IV. The Holy Scriptures
    We believe in the plenary inspiration of the Holy Scriptures . . .

V. Sin, Original and Personal
    We believe that sin came into the world through the disobedience of our first parents, and death by

sin. We believe that sin is of two kinds: original sin or depravity, and actual or personal sin. . . .

VI. *Atonement*

We believe that Jesus Christ . . . made a full atonement for all human sin, and that this Atonement is the only ground of salvation . . .

VII. *Free Agency*

We believe that the human race's creation in Godlikeness included ability to choose between right and wrong, and that thus human beings were made morally responsible . . .

VIII. *Repentance*

We believe that repentance . . . is a sincere and thorough change of the mind in regard to sin . . .

IX. *Justification, Regeneration, and Adoption*

We believe that justification . . . grants full pardon of all guilt and complete release from the penalty of sins committed . . . We believe that regeneration, or the new birth, is that gracious work of God whereby the moral nature . . . is spiritually quickened . . . We believe that adoption is that gracious act of God by which . . . [the person] is constituted a son of God. We believe that justification, regeneration, and adoption are simultaneous . . .

X. *Entire Sanctification*

We believe that entire sanctification is that act of God, subsequent to regeneration, by which believers are made free from original sin . . . love made perfect. . . .

XI. *The Church*

We believe in the Church . . . the Body of Christ called together by the Holy Spirit through the Word. . . .

XII. Baptism
We believe that Christian baptism, commanded by our Lord, is a sacrament . . . a symbol of the new covenant . . .

XIII. The Lord's Supper
We believe that the Memorial and Communion Supper instituted by our Lord . . . is essentially a New Testament sacrament . . .

XIV. Divine Healing
We believe in the Bible doctrine of divine healing and urge our people to seek to offer the prayer of faith for the healing of the sick. . . .

XV. Second Coming of Christ
We believe that the Lord Jesus Christ will come again . . .

XVI. Resurrection, Judgment, and Destiny
We believe in the resurrection of the dead . . . in future judgment . . . and everlasting life . . . to all who savingly believe in, and obediently follow, Jesus Christ our Lord; and that the finally impenitent shall suffer eternally in hell. . . . (1-22)

A closing word: Any Nazarene church board members who can comfortably discuss these points of doctrine with each other and with those outside the church are board members to be desired by any congregation. They have achieved Peter's ideal of being able to give a reason for the hope within themselves.

7

A Nazarene Lifestyle

 The purpose of this chapter is to iden-tify the essentials among Nazarene ideals and standards.

FOR A LONG TIME I attended a once-a-month breakfast club that had no official name, no membership roll, and certainly—God forbid—no rules. The men who gathered for breakfast (I don't know why, but there were never any women) ate heartily, laughed heartily, talked about any-thing on their minds, celebrated each other's birthdays, sang if they felt like it, gave away door prizes, and left when they were ready to go.

This anonymous club, which thrived across the years, was a protest against all the rules and ritual of more pur-poseful groups. However, that breakfast club in the Pacific Northwest is the only organization I know of that has claimed no reason for its existence and proclaimed no values and priorities. All other organizations I have joined in all the places I have lived and worked have had state-ments of purpose with clearly defined values and rules against unacceptable behavior. Even clubs like Rotary have rules about attendance and impose fines on people who are late.

From the beginning, the Christian Church has had its *purpose,* which is to proclaim the power of the Resurrec-tion, and its *rules,* which are the Ten Commandments as refined by the New Testament. Further, the early Christians required a radical change in the Jewish believers when they changed their day of worship from Saturday, which was celebrated with a Friday night service, to Sunday morning, which was a living reminder of the Resurrection.

The Church today lives in a vastly different culture from that of the days of the Roman Empire. But the Church still has its *purposes* and its *rules*. And why shouldn't we?

The Nazarene Purpose

According to the Foreword in the *Manual,* "The Church of the Nazarene exists to serve as an instrument for advancing the kingdom of God through the preaching and teaching of the gospel throughout the world." That is the Nazarene reason for being.

Furthermore, the Church of the Nazarene has a "well-defined commission . . . to preserve and propagate Christian holiness as set forth in the Scriptures." This commission identifies the specific reason for the existence of the Church of the Nazarene.

And finally, "Our objective is a spiritual one, namely, to evangelize as a response to the Great Commission of our Lord" (p. 5). This objective determines the Nazarene method (evangelization) and motivation (obedience to the Great Commission).

Although these mission statements are good for a worldwide denominational view, church boards must find ways to adapt the mission statements in a personal way to their own local churches. Every congregation needs to find its own way to clarify its specific mission and then declare a vision for fulfilling it.

Every effective, growing church has found its clientele and claimed its niche in the community. Who is your church trying to reach? You can't save everyone. Even

Paul, with all his drive and motivation, knew it was impossible to be all things to all people.

The Agreed Statement of Belief

Persons joining the Church of the Nazarene are asked to avow an abbreviated doctrinal statement with 8, instead of 16, articles of faith. Joiners are held to only the statements that "are essential to Christian experience." The following brief statements are held "to be sufficient."

We believe:

• *"In one God—the Father, Son, and Holy Spirit"* (26.1). Nazarenes believe in the Trinity, although its mystery is difficult to understand and explain. But the Trinity is clearly a scriptural fact of faith.

• *"That the Old and New Testament Scriptures, given by plenary inspiration, contain all truth necessary to faith and Christian living"* (26.2). Nazarenes believe in the authority and inspiration of the Scripture for all truth related to full salvation but not necessarily for unrelated truth, such as when to plant crops or how to buy a car. Through the Scriptures, God may also inspire our minds to make good decisions on our own.

• *"That man is born with a fallen nature, and is, therefore, inclined to evil, and that continually"* (26.3). Nazarenes believe man is born with a sinful nature that cannot be changed by education, behavior modification techniques, or cultural conditioning. The sinful nature is changed by cleansing.

• *"That the finally impenitent are hopelessly and eternally lost"* (26.4). Nazarenes believe in a life to come with its heaven or hell. It may not be a frequent subject in sermons, but Nazarenes believe in a hell.

• *"That the atonement through Jesus Christ is for the whole human race; and that whosoever repents and believes on the Lord Jesus Christ is justified and regenerated and saved from the dominion of sin"* (26.5). Nazarenes believe Christ died for everyone. Therefore, the royal road to being "saved from the dominion of sin," to being "justified" in the sight of God, and to being personally "regenerated," is through repentance for sins and faith in Christ.

Although persons may be saved wherever they are, Nazarenes give invitations in their services and provide altars where seekers may conveniently pray.

• *"That believers are to be sanctified wholly, subsequent to regeneration, through faith in the Lord Jesus Christ"* (26.6). Nazarenes believe that as born-again Christians reorient their lives by walking in the fresh light of the Holy Spirit, a hunger develops for a deeper spiritual work. Although their sins have been forgiven, developing Christians become increasingly aware of their sinful condition. This second work of grace is both an instantaneous experience and a lifelong process. The will may be cleansed from sin, but human nature with its biological mechanisms and mental cultural conditioning is always with us. Human beings can't be cleansed from being human.

• *"That the Holy Spirit bears witness to the new birth, and also to the entire sanctification of believers"* (26.7). The Holy Spirit is a frequent theme in Nazarene testimonies and sermons. The continuing witness of His adorable presence is life's most cherished possession.

• *"That our Lord will return, the dead will be raised, and the final judgment will take place"* (26.8). Nazarenes believe in the sure return of Christ to earth. There will be an end time when the dead shall be raised up and the Judgment will occur.

Nazarene theologians are reluctant to talk dates and to be dogmatic about conditions and schedules for the Tribulation. Most are happy to leave God's calendar and schedule of events in His hands. The most important matter is to be ready. Christ is coming!

The General Rules

Dr. Phineas F. Bresee and other founding fathers in the Church of the Nazarene believed in a happy religion. A favorite dictum of Dr. Bresee's was "Get the glory down." His services were joyful, and he himself was an optimistic person, always in a hurry. He got a speeding ticket once for driving his horse and carriage too fast on Figueroa Boulevard in Los Angeles.

Dr. Bresee also believed in rules as *helps and guides* to holy living. A Nazarene was a person with a special lifestyle. To capture this way of living, the founders decided on three General Rules.

• *"FIRST. By doing that which is enjoined in the Word of God, which is our rule of both faith and practice"* (27.1).

Nazarenes have always believed in the Bible as their Authority in faith and their Guide for living. Although the seven guidelines they lifted from the Scriptures are by no means exhaustive, there is no doubt where the founders were coming from. They wanted Nazarenes to be good human beings. Goodness does not provide salvation, but salvation without goodness is unthinkable.

"(1) Loving God with all the heart, soul, mind, and strength, and one's neighbor as oneself" (27.1). Certainly no Nazarene can resist that rule of life.

"(2) Pressing upon the attention of the unsaved the claims of the gospel, inviting them to the house of the Lord, and trying to compass their salvation" (27.1). Can any Nazarene do less?

"(3) Being courteous to all men" (27.1). Courtesy is like the air in an inflatable cushion: there is nothing to it, but it makes life easier.

"(4) Being helpful . . . in love forbearing one another"

(27.1). If there is a code of Christian decency, this rule of living must be included. If God is love and Christians are to be known by their love for each other, then mutual helpfulness is a natural.

"(5) Seeking to do good to the bodies and souls of men; feeding the hungry, clothing the naked, visiting the sick and imprisoned, and ministering to the needy, as opportunity and ability are given" (27.1). From the beginning, Nazarenes have been interested in skid row missions that feed, clothe, and house the homeless. In the Church of the Nazarene, ministering to the needs of the more unfortunate is no passing fad.

"(6) Contributing . . . in tithes and offerings" (27.1). Nazarenes are a giving people who take the offering plate seriously. Christian giving is a very important part of Christian living. One assignment of the board is to challenge the congregation to a standard of stewardship that begins with tithing—and board members must set the example.

"(7) Attending faithfully all the ordinances of God, and the means of grace, including the public worship of God . . . the sacrament of the Lord's Supper . . . searching the Scriptures . . . family and private devotions" (27.1). Nazarenes like to go to church. In many places, the Sunday evening services and Wednesday night gatherings are flourishing. Systematic personal devotions take more discipline, but Nazarenes certainly believe in a daily quiet time for prayer, reading, and just being with God.

• *"SECOND. By avoiding evil of every kind"* (27.2).

The second General Rule for Nazarenes is restrictive—what not to do. In a culture that is continually pushing its limits on personal rights, restrictive guidelines are suspect. However, the eight restrictions in these General Rules are compatible with the purpose of helping Nazarenes avoid evil that defames their character and dilutes their influence. For great numbers of people who take their Christian lifestyle seriously, these rules are no burden.

"(1) Taking the name of God in vain" (27.2). Nazarenes are offended by persons who use the name of God and His Son, Jesus Christ, in profane oaths.

"(2) Profaning of the Lord's Day" (27.2). Nazarenes believe the Sabbath can be broken in three ways: *(a)* It can be broken on Saturday night by behavior and late hours that preclude worshiping on Sunday; *(b)* it can be broken by secularizing and trivializing the Lord's day; and *(c)* it can be broken by failing to attend the means of grace on Sunday.

"(3) Sexual immorality" (27.2). The theologian Harnack has pointed out that the early Christians distinguished themselves in two ways: *(a)* They insisted—even the slave girls—on keeping themselves sexually pure. A Christian young woman in the days of the Roman Empire would rather have died than give in to the lascivious demands of a man who owned or ruled her. And they did! *(b)* They accepted each other with an unconditional love that even the nonbelievers admired.

"(4) Habits or practices known to be destructive of physical and mental well-being" (27.2). Nazarenes believe the Bible concept of the body as the temple of the Holy Spirit.

"(5) Quarreling, returning evil for evil, gossiping, slandering, spreading surmises injurious to the good names of others" (27.2). If taken literally, this rule is a hard taskmaster. But as an ideal that can be attained in measure, who could object?

"(6) Dishonesty" (27.2). Nazarenes believe in honesty and abhor dishonesty. There is no trouble in identifying

flat-out lying and stealing. But lying by silence or slanting the truth for one's own purposes does not destroy this ideal. It just makes compliance much more difficult.

"*(7) The indulging of pride in dress or behavior. Our people are to dress with the Christian simplicity and modesty that become holiness*" (27.2). This rule sounds a positive chord in the minds of Nazarenes, although standards of international application are difficult to come by. We all abhor pride in others but seldom see it in ourselves, and simplicity is a value judgment. Even modesty is in the eye of the beholder. Nazarenes need to allow each other considerable latitude in following the spirit of this rule.

"*(8) Music, literature, and entertainments that dishonor God*" (27.2). I doubt that there is a Nazarene in the land who resists the principle in this rule. But unfortunately, there is the matter of personal taste, age gaps, cultural conditioning, professional judgments, and other factors that impact the application of this rule.

In my own experience, I have found it more useful to put this rule into a positive mode that says I will listen to music, read books and magazines, and enjoy entertainments that honor God in my heart and improve my mind.

- "*THIRD. By abiding in hearty fellowship with the church, not inveighing against but wholly committed to its doctrines and usages*" (27.3).

The third and final General Rule for Nazarenes is not expanded into specific rules. However, the Board of General Superintendents has from time to time issued statements on matters that inveigh against the well-being of the church. (The dictionary says *inveigh* comes from the Latin word that means "to attack" and is pronounced *in-vay.*)

Organization and Government

The Church of the Nazarene functions well with a representative form of government that, as indicated at the beginning, depends on strong clergy leadership but gives the people the last word. This concept works at the local, district, and general levels of church governance.

(1) *"The Church of the Nazarene has a representative form of government"* (28).

In the *local* church, the congregation elects their representatives to the church board, who work with the pastor in leading and administering the church.

At the *district* level, the church sends their representatives to the district assembly, where further elections are held for representatives who serve on the various governing boards under the leadership of the district superintendent.

At the *general* level, delegates from the districts meet quadrennially for the General Assembly, which is the supreme policy-making body of the denomination. The General Assembly elects representatives who work with the Board of General Superintendents and headquarters personnel in the general administration of the denomination.

The Nazarene *institutions of higher education* are led by a cadre of strong presidents who work under the authority of boards that are chosen by the assemblies and represent the people.

(2) *"We are agreed on the necessity of a superintendency that shall complement and assist the local church in the fulfilling of its mission and objectives"* (28.1).

According to the *Manual*, the purpose of the superintendent, district or general, is to *(a)* build morale, *(b)* provide motivation, *(c)* supply management assistance, and *(d)* organize new congregations everywhere.

(3) *"We are agreed that authority given to superintendents shall not interfere with the independent action of a fully organized church"* (28.2).

The local church selects its own pastor, elects delegates to the district assemblies, manages its own finances, and has charge of all other matters pertaining to its local life and work. The relationship of the church board with the leadership of the pastor is fundamental in the functioning of a Nazarene congregation.

Special Rules

Besides the General Rules, the *Manual of the Church of the Nazarene* has a section on Special Rules. In earlier days these were called Advices. However, as the secularization of the culture gained momentum, successive General Assemblies have taken stands on issues they felt are important to a Nazarene lifestyle and made them a part of the Special Rules of the church.

Although there is not time or space in this brief guide to expound on each of these rules, an appropriate time and place should be chosen for the church board to review this section of the *Manual* in light of their own congregation. The topics discussed in the *Manual* are as follows:

(1) The Christian Life
(2) Marriage and Divorce and/or Dissolution of Marriage
(3) Abortion
(4) Human Sexuality
(5) Christian Stewardship
(6) Church Officers
(7) Rules of Order
(8) Amending Special Rules

Current Moral and Social Issues

In the back of the *Manual* are the official stands the Church of the Nazarene has taken on current moral and social issues. Although the local church board would use time wisely in reviewing this material, it is important most of all because these paragraphs demonstrate the concern of the church for current cultural issues. The Church of the Nazarene does not exist in a cocoon. It does not serve the purposes of this guide to deal with each one of these societal concerns, but for your own discussion, here they are by title:

(1) Sanctity of Human Life
(2) Organ Donation
(3) Discrimination
(4) Abuse of the Unempowered
(5) Responsibility to the Poor
(6) Women in Ministry
(7) The Church and Human Freedom
(8) War and Military Service
(9) Creation
(10) Evidence of Baptism with the Holy Spirit
(11) Magazines, Literature, Radio, and Other Media
(12) Pornography
(13) Public Swimming and Recreational Activities
(14) Substance Abuse
(15) Alcohol Desocialization
(16) Tobacco Use and Advertising

A summary word: Some church boards may feel the material in this chapter is not worthy of the space it occupies. It may be old material for many. But for all of us there is a need to be reminded of the ideas and standards of the church we love.

8

The Story of Your Church

The purpose of this chapter is to explain the meaning of a church story.

BACK OF EVERY CHURCH on every corner in America and around the world is a story. Most of the stories are captivating accounts of vision, sacrifice, miracles, and biographical sketches of some of the best people on earth.

The story line for your church may be contained within the current generation, or it may have its origins 50 or 75 or more years ago. The point is that every church has its story, and it is important for board members and pastors to know that story very well. Also, it doesn't matter whether the congregation is large or small—the story is there, and it will inform the present leadership.

No incoming pastor or church board member can expect to get along well and do effective work unless time is taken to search out the story of the church. As much as possible, the story needs to be heard from the lips of those who were there. The local church story is so important to the ongoing of the congregation that it would be well to tape the episodes and remarks of those who made a contribution to its telling.

Every story needs four contributing segments that interact with each other: (1) background, (2) main characters, (3) supporting cast, and (4) story line. These four factors are present in the story of every local church, denomination, or movement, and even in the broader history of the Christian Church.

The Story of the Local Congregation

It is especially important for every church board member to know the story of his or her own local church. After all, others have written their chapters in the continuing saga. Still more will make their contributions in the future. The present is like a single chapter in a true story that is not finished. It is a chapter that is greatly to be enjoyed, but only one of many that have been and will be.

The present board needs to keep their chapter in perspective. Present leadership is neither the beginning nor the end of the story. In fact, the end of the story will be in heaven, where all the people in the story can compare notes.

No pastor can understand a local church unless he or she has taken time to learn the local story. Besides that, it is dangerous *not* to know.

What was the community and the local culture like when the church was planted? Who were the chief characters in the development of the local church? Are they or their relatives and descendants still around? What is the story line, especially the major turning points in the history of the congregation?

The Nazarene Story

Besides knowing the story of their local church, every board member needs to know the story of the Church of the Nazarene. Why was the Church of the Nazarene born? What was happening in the churches of America that made the new denomination necessary? Who were the men and women who really made things happen in those early days? Any board member who does not know the denominational story is like a sailor who does not know his ship.

Church History at a Glance

A.D. 30—The Christian Church was born on Pentecost Sunday, when approximately 120 followers of Jesus gathered for a service in the Upper Room.

313—After nearly 300 years of misunderstanding and persecution under the Romans, the Emperor Constantine granted full toleration to the Christians. Eventually Christianity was declared the official religion of the Roman Empire. The Church took the monolithic structure of the Roman Empire with its emperor and in its ecclesiastical structure replaced him with a pope, thus paving the way for the birth of the Roman Catholic Church.

1517—Martin Luther nailed his list of 95 questions, called theses, on the door of a church in Wittenberg. As a result, discussions were opened and events began happening that resulted in the Protestant Reformation and the Counter-Reformation in the Catholic Church. Luther did away with the mass in favor of a new kind of worship, which featured the sermon, congregational singing, and the Lord's Supper. He gave the people the Bible in their own language. Most of all, he introduced again to Christianity the emphasis on salvation by grace and the priesthood of every believer. The newly invented printing press was Luther's useful ally.

1738—John Wesley's heart was "strangely warmed" during a small-group gathering on Aldersgate Street in London. He and his brother Charles were two of the major persons God used in a spiritual revival that swept England and eventually leaped across the Atlantic to America, giving birth to Methodism under Francis Asbury. Wesley was a preacher, an evangelist, a pragmatic theologian, and an organizational genius. His class meetings were the forebears of the small-group movement in America today. His concept of love perfected in holiness was a distinguishing doctrinal contribution to the church. If not our father, John Wesley was the grandfather of the Holiness Movement in America.

1838—One hundred years after John Wesley's conversion, Phineas F. Bresee was born in upstate New York. He was converted as a teenager and began preaching almost immediately. Following a sojourn in Iowa, Bresee rented a boxcar—a deluxe way to travel across country—and took his family and all their belongings to California. After a series of successful pastorates in Los Angeles and Pasadena, Bresee left the Methodist Church at 55 years of age to give the rest of his life to preaching holiness and ministering to the working classes and the poor. After a year in mission work, Bresee gathered his followers together in a storefront building in Los Angeles, where they approved their charter as a nonprofit corporation in the State of California. The first Church of the Nazarene in the West was born. The year was 1895.

1907—During the closing years of the 19th century, other Holiness bodies besides the Church of the Nazarene in Los Angeles were also founded and were actively pursuing their work. One was the Pentecostal Church of America. It began in Providence, Rhode Island, in 1887 under the leadership of Fred A. Hillery. In 1894 businessman William Howard Hoople founded a mission in Brooklyn, which became the Utica Avenue Pentecostal Tabernacle. Two more churches, Bedford Avenue Pentecostal Church and Emmanuel Pentecostal Tabernacle, were organized in New York the following year. In 1895, the same year Bresee began his work in Los Angeles, these three congregations became the Association of Pentecostal Churches of America. Under this same banner, Hillery and Hoople merged their work in 1896.

At the same time, Holiness churches were developing

on the Atlantic and Pacific coasts, while another group of churches with like doctrine was being founded in the South. They came together under the name Holiness Church of Christ.

In 1907 the churches from the East, the Association of Pentecostal Churches of America, and the churches from the West, the Church of the Nazarene, came together in Chicago to become the Pentecostal Church of the Nazarene. Two leaders—one from each group, Hiram F. Reynolds and Phineas F. Bresee—were elected general superintendents. The Southerners, the Holiness Church of Christ, sent delegates but did not join in the merger.

1908—One year later, in October 1908, the Second General Assembly of the Pentecostal Church of the Nazarene was held in Pilot Point, Texas, and a merger was completed with the southern group, including a contingent of Texans who were to provide strong second-generation leadership for the new denomination. The denomination had 10,000 members from coast to coast and an overflowing abundance of spiritual enthusiasm.

1919—Because of a groundswell of concern, the General Assembly changed the name of the organization to Church of the Nazarene because of new meanings associated with the word Pentecostal.

*　　*　　*

Interesting books are available through the Nazarene Publishing House on the lives of Nazarene leaders—from Reynolds and Bresee to the late Charles H. Strickland—plus a two-volume work on its history, *Called unto Holiness,* by Timothy L. Smith and W. T. Purkiser. Significant biographies of Bresee include E. A. Girvin's *Prince in Israel* (1916) and Carl Bangs's 1995 release.